POISONOUS SNAKES

Design
David West
Children's Book Design
Illustrations
Louise Nevett
Tessa Barwick
Picture Research
Cecilia Weston-Baker
Editor
Kate Petty

© Aladdin Books Ltd

Designed and produced by
Aladdin Books Ltd
70 Old Compton Street
London W1

First published in the
United States in 1987 by
Gloucester Press
387 Park Avenue South
New York NY 10016

ISBN 0-531-17053-5
Library of Congress Catalog
Printed in Belgium   Card Number 87-80464

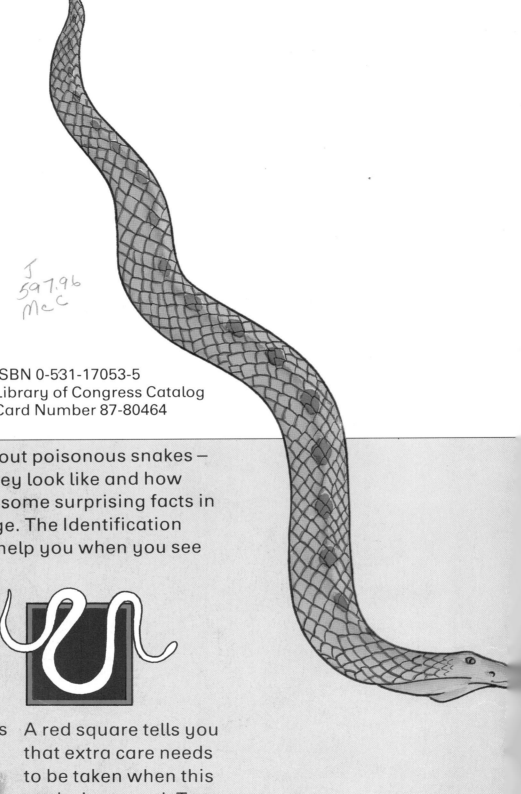

This book tells you about poisonous snakes —
how they live, what they look like and how
they survive. Find out some surprising facts in
the boxes on each page. The Identification
Chart at the back will help you when you see
snakes in the zoo.

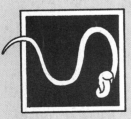 or

The little square shows
you the size of the
snake. Each side
represents about
three feet (1m).

A red square tells you
that extra care needs
to be taken when this
snake is around. Turn
to the Survival File.

The picture opposite shows a Puff Adder with its young

ꙮFIRST SIGHTꙮ
POISONOUS SNAKES

Colin McCarthy

GLOUCESTER PRESS

New York · London · Toronto · Sydney

Introduction

Poisonous snakes use poison to kill their prey.
Other snakes are constrictors, which coil themselves
around their victims to kill them. A few very
dangerous poisonous snakes do kill people, but most
snakes are not harmful to humans and there is
no need to fear them.

Even dangerous snakes are fascinating animals that
bring benefits as well as harm. In some places they
keep down the numbers of rodents and other pests.
Scientists are learning more about human nerves and
blood by studying the snake venoms which attack them.

It is best to treat all snakes with respect and to take
extra care when walking in places where snakes live.

Contents

◁ **Puff Adders are hard to see when they lie still**

How poisonous?

A poisonous snake uses its venom to kill its prey. If it has caught a rat or a bird, it injects the right amount of venom to kill an animal of that size.

Even newly hatched snakes emerge ready to catch food for themselves. These tiny poisonous snakes arrive with enough venom to kill four mice.

The King Cobra is the longest poisonous snake of all. It can grow up to 16 feet (5m). It feeds on other snakes, but it is particularly dangerous to humans because it can inject large quantities of venom when it chooses. The Indian Cobra is smaller but it bites more people because it is found near villages.

**Baby snakes emerging from their shells
ready to take care of themselves**

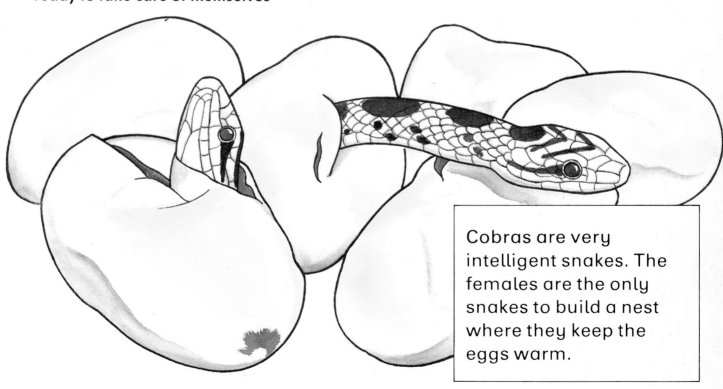

Cobras are very intelligent snakes. The females are the only snakes to build a nest where they keep the eggs warm.

◁ **The King Cobra rears up when alarmed**

Venom

Venom is the mixture of poisonous substances that these snakes use to kill their prey. It is produced in special glands that lie between the snake's eye and the corner of its mouth. Some of the poisons work on the victim's blood. Others attack its nerves and heart. The venom kills the prey, or at least stops it from moving. It also makes it easier for the snake to digest.

Venom is injected through the snake's fangs. Rear-fanged snakes have short, grooved fangs at the back of the upper jaw. In vipers and cobras the venom flows through hollow fangs at the front of the mouth. Cobras have "fixed" front fangs. Vipers have longer front fangs that fold in when not in use.

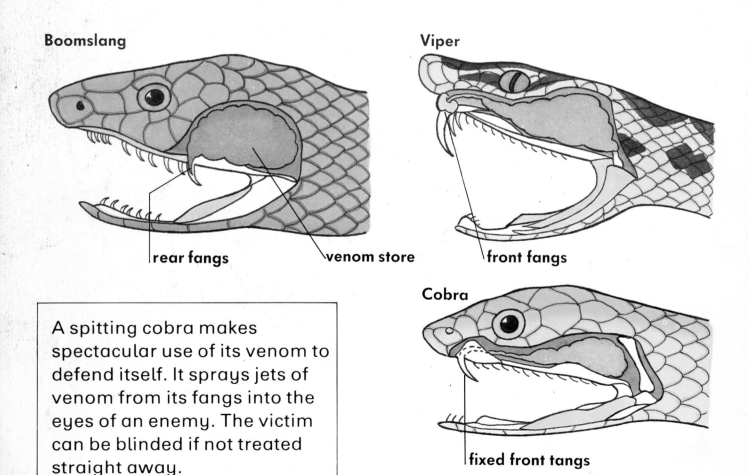

Boomslang

rear fangs

venom store

Viper

front fangs

Cobra

fixed front tangs

A spitting cobra makes spectacular use of its venom to defend itself. It sprays jets of venom from its fangs into the eyes of an enemy. The victim can be blinded if not treated straight away.

Black-necked Spitting Cobra spraying venom ▷

A bite to eat

Once a snake has a good grip on its victim it swallows it whole, even though the prey sometimes looks impossibly large. This is because the lower jaws are connected to the skull by hinge-like bones that allow the snake to open its mouth very wide. The ligament stretching between each side of the lower jaw is also very elastic. It can sometimes take a snake about an hour to swallow a large animal.

The European Adder below feeds on small mammals and frogs. It is a small viper that is found all over Europe, even in cold places. Its bite is not usually serious to humans. The Horned Adder is a desert snake that feeds on small mammals and lizards. It moves sideways across the sand.

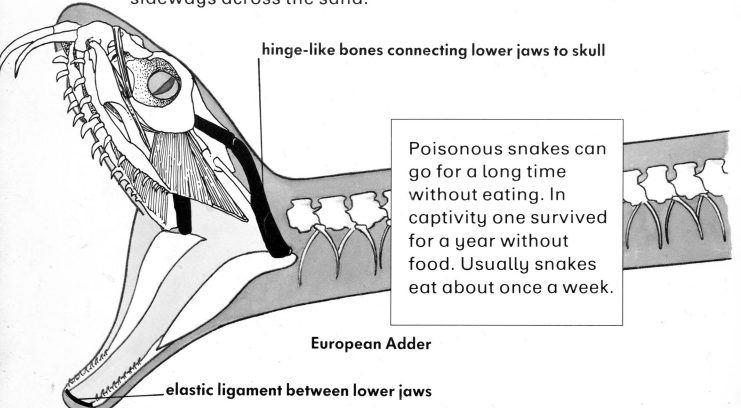

hinge-like bones connecting lower jaws to skull

Poisonous snakes can go for a long time without eating. In captivity one survived for a year without food. Usually snakes eat about once a week.

European Adder

elastic ligament between lower jaws

A Horned Adder from Namibia swallowing a mouse ▷

Rear-fanged snakes

Most rear-fanged snakes are completely harmless to humans. Their venom isn't powerful and their fangs are too short to pierce the skin. They need to get a good grip and then chew on their prey to inject the venom. They only produce a small amount of poison.

The Boomslang, a rear-fanged tree snake from Africa, is an exception. It is highly poisonous and has been known to kill people, although it usually hunts birds.

The Malayan Golden Tree Snake, also rear-fanged, is a "flying snake." Flying snakes can glide from tree to tree. They spread their ribs to make a curved surface which gives them lift, like the wings of an airplane.

The Malayan Golden Tree Snake is not harmful to humans

A famous snake specialist, Karl P. Schmidt, was killed in 1957 when a Boomslang bit him. Up until then it had been considered relatively harmless.

◁ **Boomslang eating a bird**

Cobras and their relatives

Snakes with fixed front fangs – cobras and their relatives – live in warm parts of the world. Cobras rear up when they are alarmed. They spread the loose skin on their necks into a hood. Any bite from a member of the cobra family can be serious.

Kraits and Mambas are cobra relatives. Kraits live in Asia. They are mainly active at night and feed on other snakes. Mambas live in Africa. The highly poisonous Taipans and Tiger Snakes are cobra relatives found in Australia.

Mambas live mostly in trees but the much-feared Black Mamba is often found on the ground. Mambas are the fastest snakes in the world. They can move at nine mph (15kph), as fast as a ten-year-old runner.

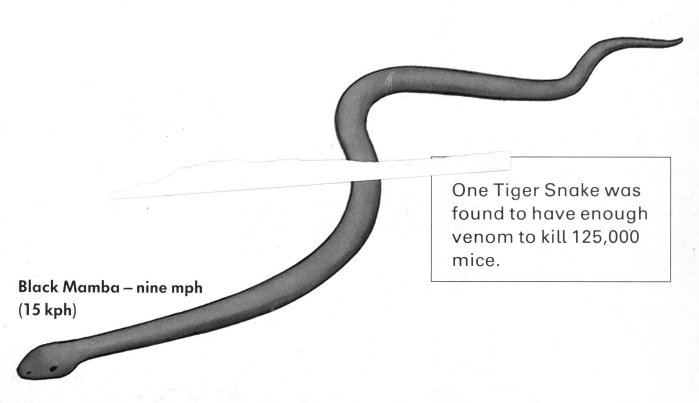

One Tiger Snake was found to have enough venom to kill 125,000 mice.

Black Mamba – nine mph (15 kph)

◁ **A Black Mamba on the ground**

This little rhyme tells the difference between a coral snake and a harmless mimic: Red touch yellow, bad for a fellow; Red touch black, good for Jack.

American Coral Snake

Scarlet King Snake

Warning signals

The colorful coral snakes are the only cobra relatives in the Americas. They also live in Africa and Asia. They usually have a very clear pattern of yellow, black and red bands, which makes them easily seen. The pattern is a warning signal that the snake is dangerous and should be left alone. Coral snakes are very poisonous. Many of their victims are young children who pick them up because they are so pretty and seem very quiet.

There are other, harmless snakes that look like coral snakes. They fool their enemies into thinking they are dangerous, so they stay away.

Vipers

There are about 170 species of viper. They live in almost all the countries of the world except for Australia. Vipers have wide, triangular-shaped heads. They have a very efficient way of injecting venom into their prey. When a viper attacks a mouse, for example, it opens its mouth wide, swings its fangs into the upright position and strikes with great speed. As soon as the venom has been injected, the viper releases the mouse. The mouse is not killed immediately and often crawls away. The viper soon tracks it down by its scent. Adders are vipers. The Puff Adder and the Gaboon Viper are both found in Africa.

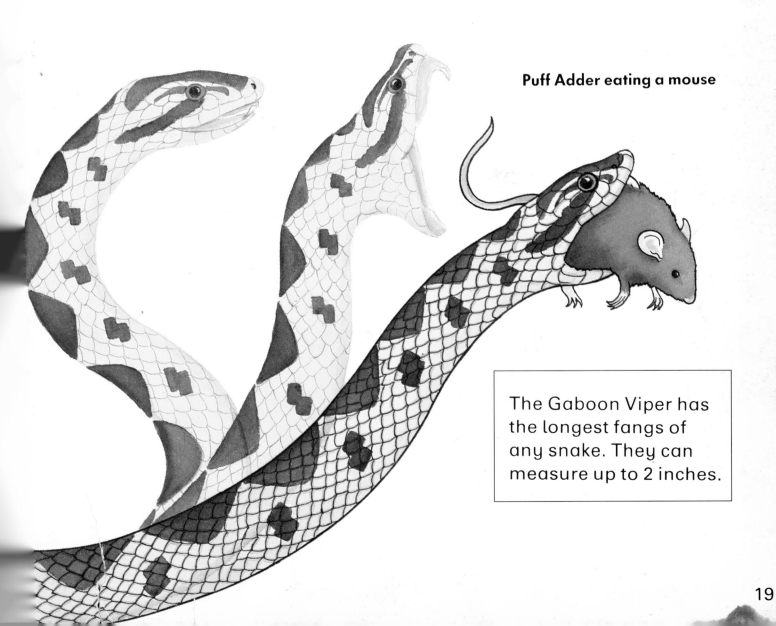

Puff Adder eating a mouse

The Gaboon Viper has the longest fangs of any snake. They can measure up to 2 inches.

Snake senses

Most snakes have poor sight and poor hearing. Their sense of smell, though, is excellent. The organs that detect smell are on the roof of the snake's mouth. Scent particles are transferred there by the snake's flicking tongue. Some snakes, called pit vipers, can also sense the body heat of their prey through special heat receptors, or "pits." They can be seen midway between the nostrils and the eyes. These pits are sensitive to any warm object. The snake can strike accurately at its prey, even in the dark.

One of the most deadly pit vipers is the Bushmaster from South America. Luckily it is shy and rarely seen.

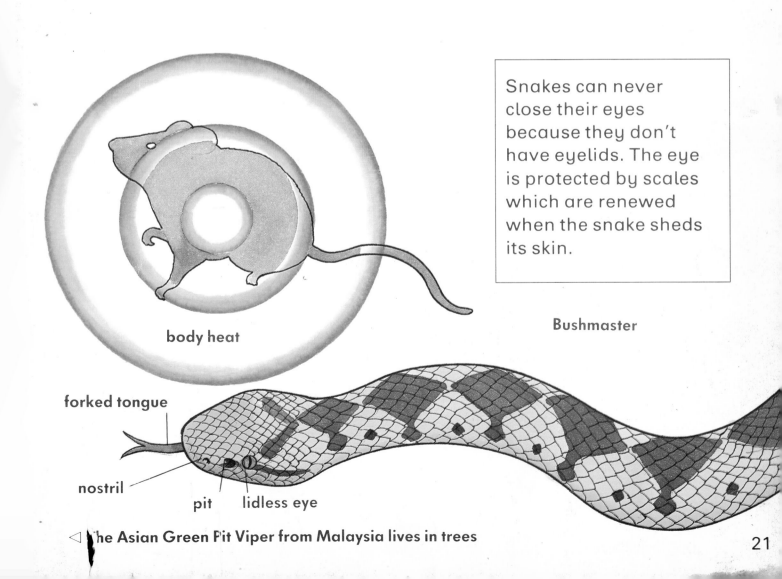

body heat

Snakes can never close their eyes because they don't have eyelids. The eye is protected by scales which are renewed when the snake sheds its skin.

Bushmaster

forked tongue

nostril

pit   lidless eye

◁ The Asian Green Pit Viper from Malaysia lives in trees

Rattlesnakes

Rattlesnakes are pit vipers. There are about 30 species of them living in the United States. The most remarkable thing about these snakes is the rattle on the end of the tail. A rattlesnake waves its tail when it is alarmed. It makes a whirring, crackling noise when it is shaken. The sound of the rattle warns any animal that might try to attack the snake or accidentally step on it.

Diamondback rattlesnakes are the most deadly snakes in the United States. Rattlesnakes usually strike from a coiled position, lunging forward up to two-thirds of their length. They can act very quickly — the Western Diamondback strikes at a speed of ten feet (3.5m) per second.

A Diamondback's rattle

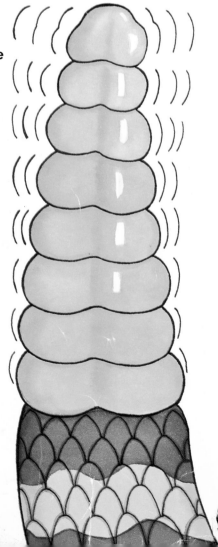

The rattle is made of hollow, loosely linked segments. A new segment is added each time the snake sheds its skin, perhaps four or five times a year. Counting them can give a very rough idea of the snake's age.

Sea snakes

There are many myths and superstitions surrounding sea snakes, the sea serpents of legend. Sailors were supposed to hear the wail of a sea serpent whenever a ship was wrecked.

There are about 50 species of sea snakes living in the warm tropical seas around southern Asia and northern Australia. Their tails are flattened like paddles. Their nostrils are on top of the snout so most of the snake is hidden underwater even when it comes up for air. Many never come out of the water. Only Sea Kraits come ashore to lay their eggs. Others produce live babies at sea. Sea snakes feed mainly on fish. They are highly poisonous – one of them has venom a hundred times more potent than that of a land snake.

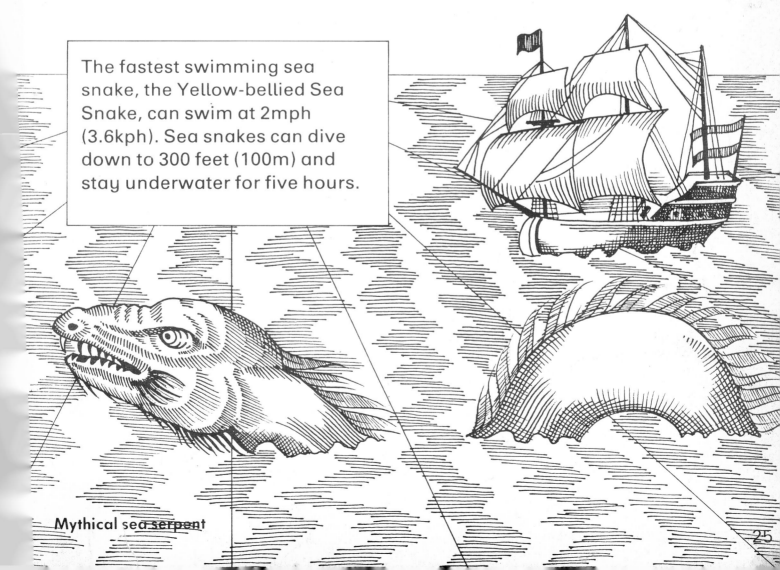

The fastest swimming sea snake, the Yellow-bellied Sea Snake, can swim at 2mph (3.6kph). Sea snakes can dive down to 300 feet (100m) and stay underwater for five hours.

Mythical sea serpent

Snake enemies

Snakes have a number of enemies. They are not even safe from their own kind – the huge King Cobra from Asia feeds almost entirely on other snakes. Birds of prey such as eagles, hawks, owls and Secretary Birds will kill and eat snakes. The little mongoose is one of the best known snake-killers. Usually a mongoose avoids challenging a large cobra, but if there is a fight the mongoose is more likely to win. The snake is no match for the speed, agility and sharp teeth of the mongoose.

Humans are probably the greatest threat to snakes, often killing them unnecessarily, out of fear. People also kill them for their skins, which can be sold for a lot of money.

It takes about eight snakeskins to make a purse that costs $150 in stores.

Secretary Bird trampling a snake

Survival file

Although snake bites kill about 30,000 people every year worldwide, in most places the risk of death is very small. Most victims are farmers who work barefoot in tropical places where hospitals are hard to reach.

You should always take care when walking in areas where snakes are known to live. Don't poke about in places where they like to hide. If someone does get bitten they will probably need to be treated with antivenom.

Demonstration of snake-handling for schoolchildren

The Indian Cobra is found near villages in Southern Asia so people quite often get bitten. Snake farms "milk" cobras for their venom. Large quantities of venom are needed to prepare the antivenom.

The Black Mamba from Africa tries to flee when approached. If its escape route is blocked it rears up and opens its jaws. Any sudden movement will cause it to strike. Victims need antivenom right away.

Puff Adders are common in African countries. They hiss loudly when alarmed. They move slowly and usually stay still when approached. People get bitten when they walk on or near a Puff Adder accidentally.

As one of the few northern European snakes, the European Adder is in need of protection. Its habitat is gradually disappearing and it is often killed needlessly.

Some people in the United States are bitten by Diamondback Rattlesnakes, but only a few die. Some victims are more sensitive to snake venoms than others.

Fangs of a Diamondback Rattlesnake

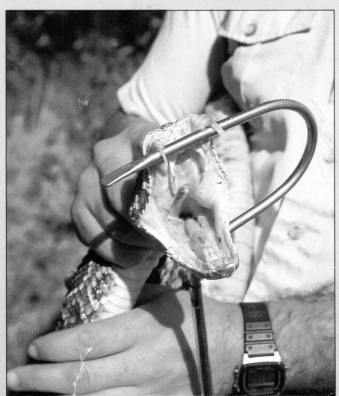

Black Tiger snake being "milked" for venom

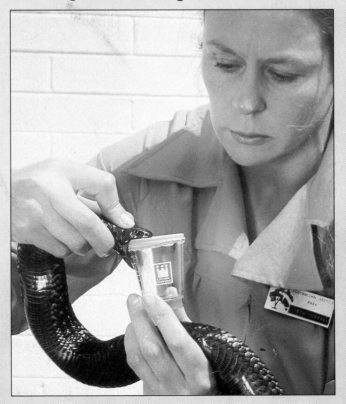

Identification chart

This chart shows you some of the poisonous snakes to watch for in zoos or in the outdoors, if you are in snake country. They are drawn to scale to show their comparative sizes. The sides of each square on the grid represent six inches (15cm).

- ◐ N. America
- ● S. America
- ◐ Europe
- ◐ Africa
- ◐ Asia
- ○ Australia

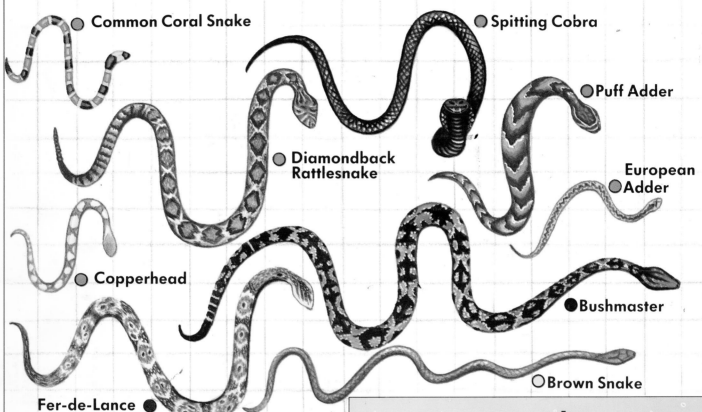

- ◐ Common Coral Snake
- ◐ Spitting Cobra
- ◐ Puff Adder
- ◐ Diamondback Rattlesnake
- ◐ European Adder
- ◐ Copperhead
- ● Bushmaster
- ○ Brown Snake
- ● Fer-de-Lance

Make a coiled snake

1. Draw your snake on thin board.
2. Color it in, using the chart.
3. Cut around the spiral.
4. Now you have a coiled snake.
5. Balance the snake on a ballpoint pen fixed to a radiator. The warm air will make it turn around.

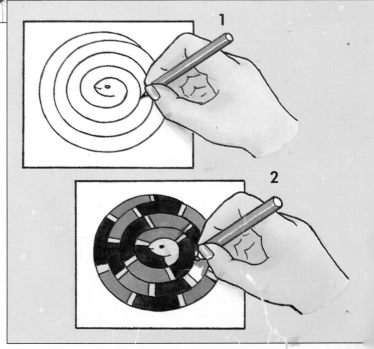

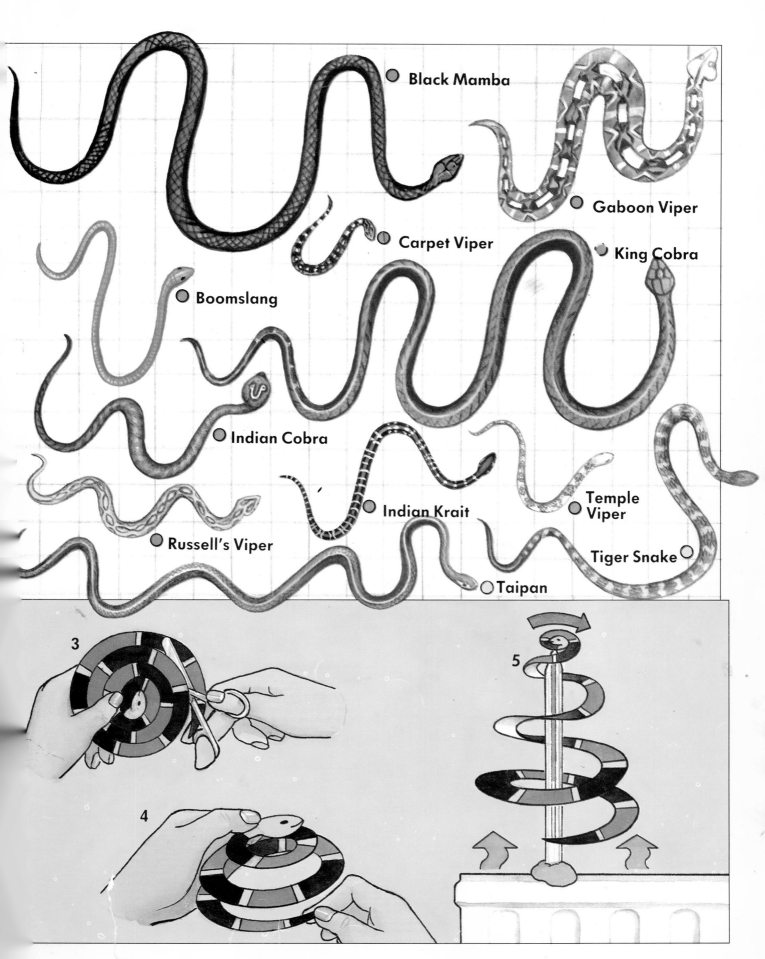

Black Mamba

Gaboon Viper

Carpet Viper

King Cobra

Boomslang

Indian Cobra

Temple Viper

Russell's Viper

Indian Krait

Tiger Snake

Taipan

3

4

5

Index

The picture on the cover shows a Green Pit Viper

Photographic credits: Cover, title page, contents page and pages 10, 14, 16, 20, 24, 26 and 31 (top): Bruce Coleman; page 6: Planet Earth; page 8 and 31 (bottom): NHPA; pages 12 and 22: Survival Anglia; page 18: David & Eric Hosking; page 30: Sdeuard Bisserôt.

PRINTED IN BELGIUM BY

proost
INTERNATIONAL BOOK PRODUCTION